Real People

Abraham Lincoln

By Pamela Walker

Children's Press
A Division of Scholastic Inc.
New York / Toronto / London / Auckland / Sydney
Mexico City / New Delhi / Hong Kong
Danbury, Connecticut

Photo Credits: Cover, pp. 13 (0-93), 15 (0-92c), 17 (0-65), 19 (0-88), Courtesy of The Lincoln Museum, Fort Wayne, IN; p. 5 © Medford Historical Society collection/Corbis; p. 7 © Morton Beebe/Corbis; p. 9 © Bettman/Corbis; p. 11 © AP/Photo; p. 21 © Wolfgang/Kaehler/Corbis
Contributing Editors: Jeri Cipriano, Jennifer Silate
Book Design: Christopher Logan

Visit Children's Press on the Internet at:
http://publishing.grolier.com

Library of Congress Cataloging-in-Publication Data

Walker, Pam, 1958-
   Abraham Lincoln / by Pamela Walker.
     p. cm. — (Real people)
   Includes bibliographical references and index.
   ISBN 0-516-23432-3 (lib. bdg.) — ISBN 0-516-23586-9 (pbk.)
      1. Lincoln, Abraham, 1809-1865—Juvenile literature. 2. Lincoln, Abraham, 1809-1865—Pictorial works—Juvenile literature. 3. Presidents—United States—Biography—Juvenile literature. [1. Lincoln, Abraham, 1809-1865. 2. Presidents.]
   I. Title.

E457.905 .W33 2001
973.7'092—dc21
[B]
                                                                    00-065622

Contents

This is Abraham Lincoln.

He was the 16th **president** of the United States.

5

Abe was born in 1809.

As a boy, he lived in a **log cabin**.

Abe always worked hard.

9

Abraham Lincoln was **married** to Mary Todd.

They had a family together.

11

Abe loved his family and he loved to read.

He read books with his son, Tad.

13

Abe became the president of the United States.

15

A **war** started **between**
the states.

Abe worked hard
to end the war.

17

Many people think that he was a great president.

Today, we can see Abe's face on a penny.

There are **statues** to remember him.

We will never forget Abraham Lincoln.

IN THIS TEMPLE
AS IN THE HEARTS OF THE PEOPLE
FOR WHOM HE SAVED THE UNION
THE MEMORY OF ABRAHAM LINCOLN
IS ENSHRINED FOREVER

21

New Words

between (bih-**tween**) having to do with

log cabin (**log kab**-ihn) a small house made of logs

married (**mar**-eed) living together as husband and wife

president (**prehz**-uh-duhnt) the person elected to be in charge of the nation

statues (**stach**-ooz) stone, wood, or metal objects that are made to look like people

war (**wor**) a fight between states or countries

To Find Out More

Books
A Picture Book of Abraham Lincoln
by David A. Adler
Holiday House

Abraham Lincoln
by Ingri D'Aulaire and Edgar Parin D'Aulaire
Dell Publishing

Web Sites
Abraham Lincoln Online
http://showcase.netins.net/web/creative/lincoln/tours/tourhome.htm
This site offers photo tours of places where Abraham Lincoln lived
and worked.

The Life of Abraham Lincoln
http://www.berwickacademy.org/lincoln/lincoln.htm
The life of Abraham Lincoln is illustrated in a time line created
for and by young readers.

Index

About the Author

Pamela Walker was born in Kentucky. When she grew up, she moved to New York and became a writer.

Reading Consultants

Kris Flynn, Coordinator, Small School District Literacy, The San Diego County Office of Education

Shelly Forys, Certified Reading Recovery Specialist, W.J. Zahnow Elementary School, Waterloo, IL

Sue McAdams, Certified Reading Recovery Specialist and Literary Consultant, Dallas, TX